First World War
and Army of Occupation
War Diary
France, Belgium and Germany

38 DIVISION
113 Infantry Brigade,
Brigade Trench Mortar Battery
1 January 1916 - 30 April 1916

WO95/2556/4

The Naval & Military Press Ltd
www.nmarchive.com
Published in association with The National Archives

Published by

The Naval & Military Press Ltd

Unit 10 Ridgewood Industrial Park,

Uckfield, East Sussex,

TN22 5QE England

Tel: +44 (0) 1825 749494

www.naval-military-press.com

www.nmarchive.com

This diary has been reprinted in facsimile from the original. Any imperfections are inevitably reproduced and the quality may fall short of modern type and cartographic standards.

© Crown Copyright
Images reproduced by permission of The National Archives, London, England, 2015.

Contents

Document type	Place/Title	Date From	Date To
Heading	WO95/2556/4		
Heading	113 Trench Mortar Bty 1916 Jan To 1916 Apr		
Heading	113 Trench Mortar Bty Jan Vol I 22nd Bde		
War Diary	Valheureux	01/01/1916	01/01/1916
War Diary	Warlus	08/01/1916	30/01/1916
War Diary	Vaux	31/01/1916	31/01/1916
War Diary	Querrieu	01/02/1916	01/02/1916
War Diary	Morlancourt	02/02/1916	18/03/1916
War Diary	C Sector	19/03/1916	03/04/1916
War Diary	C1 Sector	04/04/1916	06/04/1916
War Diary	C1	07/04/1916	15/04/1916
War Diary	Valheureux	16/04/1916	30/04/1916

MO95 / 3556 / 4.

~~4 Army Troops~~
38 DIV
113 BDE

113
TRENCH MORTAR
BTY

1916 JAN TO 1916 APR

2366

113/
11/3 French Motor Bly
Jan
Vol I
22nd Bde

Army Form C. 2118.

WAR DIARY
or
INTELLIGENCE=SUMMARY.
(Erase heading not required.)

115th Trench Mortar Battery.
3rd Army

Place	Date	Hour	Summary of Events and Information	Remarks and references to Appendices
	Jan			
VALHEUREUX	7.1.16	9.30 am	113th Battery proceeded from School of Mortars 3rd Army and reported to Hdqrs 22nd Inf Bde at MOULLENS-VIDAME. Billets were found at WARLUS. Brigade are at rest.	
WARLUS	8.1.16		Interior economy.	
WARLUS	9.1.16		Fatigues. Gunnery Route marches.	
	10.			
	28.1.16			
WARLUS	29.1.16		Orders received for 22nd Inf Bde to take over trenches in vicinity of ALBERT. March table for 113th T.M. Bty received from Bde Major.	
WARLUS	30.1.16	8 am	Left WARLUS for VAUX via LA CHAUSSEE - ST VAST. Billeted at VAUX for night 30/31	
VAUX	31.1.16	9 am	Left VAUX for QUERRIEU via COISY - BILLONVILLE. Billeted at QUERRIEU for night 31/1	

Army Form C. 2118.

WAR DIARY
or
INTELLIGENCE SUMMARY.
(Erase heading not required.)

113th T.M. Bty
3rd Army

Place	Date	Hour	Summary of Events and Information	Remarks and references to Appendices
	Feb			
GUERRIEU	1.2.16	9am	Bn. Querrieu to Morlancourt arrived 3 p.m.	
MORLANCOURT	3.2.16		Officer proceeded to Heuobes in Sector D1 - inspected gun positions and reported to 22nd Inf. Bde.	
MORLANCOURT	2.2.16 6.2.16		In reserve.	
MORLANCOURT	6.2.16	1 p.m.	Half battery took over from 99th T.M. Battery in D1 Sector.	
D1	7.2.16		Hostile T.M's quiet. No rounds fired.	
D1	8.2.16		Reserve positions being prepared.	
D1	9.2.16	9.30am	Retaliated with 8 rounds for this enemy T.M's.	
		6.30pm	3 " " " one " T.M.	
D1	10.2.16		16 rounds fired on enemy's reserve trenches.	
D1	11.2.16		No rounds fired. All quiet.	
D1	12.2.16	10.30am	Relieved by other half of Battery.	
D1	12.2.16	2 pm	Fired 6 rounds in retaliation for hostile T.M. which ceased fire	
D1	13.2.16	12am	Fired 8 rounds on enemy communication trenches by little retaliation	
D1	14.2.16	12.30am	Fired 8 rounds at hostile T.M. Enemy retaliated with artillery	
D1	15.2.16	4.30pm	Fired 8 rounds on German machine gun emplacement. Some damage to material was observed	

Army Form C. 2118.

WAR DIARY
or
INTELLIGENCE SUMMARY.
(Erase heading not required.)

Instructions regarding War Diaries and Intelligence Summaries are contained in F. S. Regs., Part II. and the Staff Manual respectively. Title pages will be prepared in manuscript.

Place	Date	Hour	Summary of Events and Information	Remarks and references to Appendices
D1	18/2/16	11 a.m.	Fired 5 rounds in retaliation for grenades & hostile T.M. Enemy fire ceased	
		11.30pm	Fired 6 rounds on Communication Trenches	
D1	17/2/16	11.30pm	Fired 9 rounds in retaliation for hostile T.M. Enemy fire	
	18/2/16 19/2/16	2.0 a.m.	Fired 2 rounds at Communication Trenches	
		10.30 a.m.	Retired by Section in rest.	
D1	19.2.16		Retaliated with 10 rounds for 2 enemy T.M's	
D1	20.2.16		Enemy trench mortars quiet. 4 rounds fired	
D1	21.2.16		Two rounds fired at enemy trenches. Some damage to parapet was observed.	
D1	22.2.16	6.30pm	Some hostile T.M's were fired. We retaliated with 16 rounds on enemy front line (bombardment)	
D1	23.2.16		Fifteen rounds expended.	
D1	24.2.16	9.am.	Fired six rounds	
		12 noon	Relieved by Section in rest.	
D1	25/2/16		Fired 9 rounds in retaliation for hostile mortars	
D1	26/2/16		Enemy mortars active. Fired 23 rounds in retaliation. Hostile mortars ceased firing	
D1	27/2/16		Fired 25 rounds on various points on Communication trenches. Very little retaliation	
D1	28/2/16		Fired 41 Rounds at Communication trenches. Searched & swept for hostile mortars	

Army Form C. 2118.

WAR DIARY
or
INTELLIGENCE SUMMARY.
(Erase heading not required.)

Instructions regarding War Diaries and Intelligence Summaries are contained in F. S. Regs., Part II. and the Staff Manual respectively. Title pages will be prepared in manuscript.

Place	Date	Hour	Summary of Events and Information	Remarks and references to Appendices
D.1.	29/9/16		Fired 20 Rounds in retaliation for hostile T.M.s Retaliation effective	

T/134. Wt. W708-776. 500090. 4/15. Sir J. C. & S.

Army Form C. 2118.

WAR DIARY
or
INTELLIGENCE SUMMARY.
(Erase heading not required.)

113th T.M. Battery

Instructions regarding War Diaries and Intelligence Summaries are contained in F. S. Regs., Part II. and the Staff Manual respectively. Title pages will be prepared in manuscript.

Place	Date	Hour	Summary of Events and Information	Remarks and references to Appendices
D1	1/3/16		Fired 39 Rounds in retaliation for hostile artillery and in registration at points opposite the quarry. An additional gun has been sent up.	
		11:30pm	Relieved by Section in Rest	
D1	2.3.16		12 rounds fired at German trail line.	
	3.3.16		Opened fire on suspected hostile TM positions. 30 rounds were expended.	
	4.3.16		Enemy were not very active. 16 rounds were sent over in retaliation for some hostile TMs.	
	5.3.16		18 rounds were fired at various targets in enemy supports. Damage was done to material.	
	6.3.16		Enemy sent over some TMs. Retaliation was given with 30 rounds. Enemy were silenced.	
	7.3.16		Enemy fired TMs at intervals during day. 192 retaliation on each occasion firing 61 rounds.	
	8/3/16		Battery fired 18 Rounds at Enemy's Front Line in retaliation for hostile T.M.S	
	9/3/16		Battery fired 56 Rounds on Front-line & Communication trenches. Very little retaliation was given. Bombarding Grenadiers received	

WAR DIARY or INTELLIGENCE SUMMARY

Army Form C. 2118.

113th T.M Battery

Place	Date	Hour	Summary of Events and Information	Remarks and references to Appendices
	10/3/16	1:15pm	In conjunction with the 113 Battery (Sletics) we fired on various points in the enemy's line. Enemy retaliated with heavy artillery. Ammunition expended 83 Rounds. 2/Lieut G.R. Simpson R.F.A. slightly wounded.	
	11/3/16		Battery fired 31 Rounds on enemy's front line. Enemy are systematically shelling "Wytschaete" with heavy artillery.	
	12/3/16		Battery fired 68 Rounds in retaliation for hostile mortars. Considerable damage to material was observed.	
	13/3/16		Battery fired 14 Rds in retaliation. Enemy mortars appear to have been considerably augmented and have been more active of late. Relieved by 9 Section in rest.	
	14.3.16		Quiet day. No firing. Situation normal.	
	15.3.16		Seventy rounds expended in retaliating to enemy T.M.s.	
	16.3.16		Trench mortars were active in this sector. 34 rounds fired.	
	17.3.16		Situation normal. Very few trench mortars.	
	18.3.16		36 rounds were fired at an observation post and enemy sniper position. 16 rounds expended. Ammunition was fired at action and OP greatly damaged. Damage to enemy parapet and wire visible.	

Army Form C. 2118.

WAR DIARY
or
INTELLIGENCE SUMMARY.
(Erase heading not required.)

113ᵗʰ T.M. Battery

Place	Date	Hour	Summary of Events and Information	Remarks and references to Appendices
"Q Sector" (numbering of Sector)	19.3.16		10 rounds fired. Enemy is all short of or sparing in T.M. ammunition. As a great falling off has been observed where such a large amount of T.M. fire has been experienced for a long time past.	
	20.3.16		2ⁿᵈ Lieut. Rundell arrived from T.M School to relieve 2ⁿᵈ Lieut. Simpson. 31 rounds fired at sawing pits in enemy line. Damage to material observed.	
	21.3.16		A few hostile T.M. fired. Retaliated with 18 rounds. 2ⁿᵈ Lieut. Rooke R.F.A. carried "O" replace 2ⁿᵈ Lieut. Rundell who returned to T.M.S.	
Q S.Sector	22.3.16		2ⁿᵈ Lieut. Rooke went down to relieve 2ⁿᵈ Lieut. Rundell in Trenches. 4 heavy & 20 light Bombs were fired this were observed on Enemy Sniping Posts & enemy front lines, & much damage to material was done. 2ⁿᵈ Lieut. Simpson went on leave.	
	23.3.16		Enemy active with Minnies during the day & night, established with 2 heavy & one light Bomb. Enemy sniping post was blown up.	

T/134. Wt. W708—776. 50C090. 4/15. Sir J.C. & S.

Army Form C. 2118.

WAR DIARY
or
INTELLIGENCE SUMMARY.
(Erase heading not required.)

113th T.M. Battery

Instructions regarding War Diaries and Intelligence Summaries are contained in F.S. Regs., Part II. and the Staff Manual respectively. Title pages will be prepared in manuscript.

Place	Date	Hour	Summary of Events and Information	Remarks and references to Appendices
G. Suku	24.3.16		Owing to important mining operations in progress retaliation by T M Battery was ordered to a minimum consequently ammunition expenditure was nil.	
	25.3.16		Enemy were very active this morning with rifle grenades & minenwerfer. Enemy was very active this morning at 4 a.m. with carrier. Retaliated with 8 Heavy Bombs on enemy front line. Enemy retaliated to on Trench Mortar fire with Heavy Artillery with some violence for a growth of an hour.	
		11.45"	Was relieved by Trench Mortars of this duty Battery	
	26.3.16		Shichian very quiet. No rounds fired.	
	27.3.16		Enemy fired Trench Mortars and rifle grenades at intervals. Retaliated with 51 rounds.	
	28.3.16		Quiet day. 10 rounds fired.	
	29.3.16		A few hostile T.M's came over. 10 rounds retaliation.	
	30.3.16		Enemy slightly active with rifle grenades and minenwerfer. Retaliated with 18 rounds on Front line Trenches.	
	31.3.16		Several hostile rifle grenades and T.M's. We fired 35 rounds.	

Army Form C. 2118.

WAR DIARY
or
INTELLIGENCE SUMMARY.
(Erase heading not required.)

113th T.M. Battery Vol 1

Instructions regarding War Diaries and Intelligence Summaries are contained in F. S. Regs., Part II. and the Staff Manual respectively. Title pages will be prepared in manuscript.

Place	Date	Hour	Summary of Events and Information	Remarks and references to Appendices
C Sector	1.4.16		The left half of the Battery fired 66 rounds from 6 PM 31.3.16 to 6 PM 1.4.16. Much damage was observed to enemy material & wire was cut from their trenches & were blown in & some enemy mining works were seriously damaged.	
	2.4.16	9.40 AM	Fired 5 rounds in retaliation for Enemy excessive lits were observed on enemy communication trenches.	
		2.30 PM	Fired six more rounds in retaliation for enemy T.M's. Enemy seems to be getting more Trench Mortars or more ammunition as he fires far more frequently than he used to do.	
		4 PM	A new kind of Bomb was observed this afternoon, familiarly known as a drainpipe it is about 2 feet long by 4 inches wide with wooden ends, & is made of very inferior material. Ammunition exploded on retaliation were 18 rounds, much damage was done to enemy works.	
	3.4.16	3.20 PM	One exercise was sustained by my duty Battery through a faulty fuse exploding. No. 49381 Spr Duncan was The casualty, as hand blown off.	

WAR DIARY
or
INTELLIGENCE SUMMARY.
(Erase heading not required.)

Army Form C. 2118.

Instructions regarding War Diaries and Intelligence Summaries are contained in F. S. Regs., Part II. and the Staff Manual respectively. Title pages will be prepared in manuscript.

Place	Date	Hour	Summary of Events and Information	Remarks and references to Appendices
C I Sector	4.4.16	11.30	We retaliated to enemy Trench Mortars with 7 rounds after which the enemy retaliated with enemy artillery. Shrapnel used to shell the new position the enemy having located & answered any other fire.	
		9.30 PM	We fired 4 more rounds in retaliation for enemy ravation which our dummy gun support.	
	5.4.16		Arrived. to the 5e Battery OP to observe for my Battery of T.M.s. from the 57th SP on our left. The enemy front & Second lines & communication Trenches also communication to TM position. Some very good shooting was done on the enemy front & second lines & also on some of his newer communication Trench junctions. One dugout was blown in and at Shand & Reenyie full & coals taking several shovel & flyup also being thirty much enemy were knocked in, in all 20 rounds were fired	
	6.4.16		17 rounds were fired at position located from S.e Battery OP. it is thought much damage was done, as the enemy retaliated vigorously with artillery. We have received of regeterdy of The Battery	

T.2134. Wt. W708-776. 500'000. 4/15. Sir J. C. & S.

Army Form C. 2118.

WAR DIARY
or
INTELLIGENCE SUMMARY.
(Erase heading not required.)

Instructions regarding War Diaries and Intelligence Summaries are contained in F.S. Regs., Part II. and the Staff Manual respectively. Title pages will be prepared in manuscript.

113th T.M.B.

Place	Date	Hour	Summary of Events and Information	Remarks and references to Appendices
C.	7.4.16		Enemy fired T.M.s intermittently. Retaliated with 36 rounds	
	8.4.16		Opened fire on various pts in enemy lines. 36 rounds were fired. Very little retaliation	
	9.4.16		Very quiet day. No rounds fired	
	10.4.16		A few hostile T.M. came over. On retaliating with 28 rounds enemy ceased fire.	
	11.4.16		29 rounds were fired on enemy front line and supports. No material damage was observed.	
	12.4.16		We opened fire on observation post in enemy front line. This was destroyed. A large quantity of wire was also destroyed. Later in the evening we caught enemy repairing wire. Party was dispersed.	
	13.4.16		Cornhill Battery at rest.	
	14.4.16		Battery moved 15 T.M. School 15 hand over guns and get new ones.	
	15.4.16		At School	

Army Form C. 2118.

WAR DIARY
or
INTELLIGENCE SUMMARY.
(Erase heading not required.)

11⅓ T.M.B.

Place	Date	Hour	Summary of Events and Information	Remarks and references to Appendices
VALHEUREUX	16.4.16		At School.	
	17.4.16		At School	
	18.4.16		Returned to Montauban.	
	19.4.16		At Rest.	
	23.4.16		2nd Lieut. Rooke took Battery to B sector to dig new positions.	
	28.4.16			
	29.4.16		Digging in.	
	29.4.16			
	30.4.16			

www.ingramcontent.com/pod-product-compliance
Lightning Source LLC
Chambersburg PA
CBHW081253170426
43191CB00037B/2140